EXPERIMENT!

Up, Up and Away

The Science of Flight

by Dr. David Darling

dP **DILLON PRESS**
New York

Maxwell Macmillan Canada
Toronto

Maxwell Macmillan International
New York Oxford Singapore Sydney

Photographic Acknowledgments

The photographs are reproduced through the courtesy of The Boeing Company, British Aerospace, General Electric, Goodyear, McDonnell Douglas, NASA, and Unicorn Stock Photos/Tom McCarthy, Vasco Martin, Jr., Pam Power, Charles E. Schmidt, and Herbert L. Stormont.

Library of Congress Cataloging-in-Publication Data
Darling, David J.
   Up, up, and away : the science of flight / by David Darling.
      p. cm. — (Experiment!)
   Includes index.
   Summary: Explains and demonstrates the principles of flight through experiments and provides information on different types of aircraft.
   ISBN 0-87518-479-0
   1. Flight—Juvenile literature. 2. Flight—Experiments—Juvenile literature. [1. Flight—Experiments. 2. Experiments.]
   I. Title. II. Series : Darling, David J. Experiment!
TL547.D17   1991b
629.19'09—dc20   91-4000

Dillon Press
Macmillan Publishing Company
866 Third Avenue
New York, NY 10022

Maxwell Macmillan Canada, Inc.
1200 Eglinton Avenue East
Suite 200
Don Mills, Ontario M3C 3N1

Macmillan Publishing Company is part of the Maxwell Communication Group of Companies.

First edition
Printed in the United States of America
10 9 8 7 6 5 4 3 2 1

Contents

What Is Science? 4

1 Amazing Air 9

2 Wings and Lifting Things 14

3 Plane Easy! 20

4 Flight with a Twist 34

5 Staying Up–without Really Trying 39

6 Faster and Farther 49

Experiment in Depth 53

Glossary 57

Index 59

What Is Science?

Imagine gazing to the edge of the universe with the help of a giant telescope, or designing a future car using a computer that can do over a billion calculations a second. Think what it would be like to investigate the strange calls of the humpback whale, dig up the bones of a new type of dinosaur, or drill a hole ten miles into the earth.

As you read this, men and women around the world are doing exactly these things. Others are trying to find out how the human brain works, how to build better rocket engines, and how to develop new energy sources for the twenty-first century. There are researchers working at the South Pole, in the Amazon jungle,

under the sea, in space, and in laboratories on every continent. All these people are scientists. But what does that mean? Just what is science?

Observation

Science is simply a way of looking at the world with an open, inquiring mind. It usually starts with an observation. For example, you might observe that the leaves of some trees turn brown, yellow, or red in fall. That may seem obvious. But

to a scientist, it raises all sorts of interesting questions. What substances in a leaf cause the various colors? What happens when the color changes? Does the leaf swap its green-colored chemical for a brown one? Or are the chemicals that cause the fall colors there all the time but remain hidden from view when the green substance is present?

Hypothesis

At this stage, you might come up with your own explanation for what is going on inside the leaf. This early explanation–a sort of intelligent guess–is called a working hypothesis. To be useful, a hypothesis should lead to predictions that can be tested. For instance, your hypothesis might be that leaves always contain brown, yellow, or red chemicals. It is just that when the green substance is there it masks or covers over the other colors. This is a good scientific hypothesis because a test can be done that could prove it wrong.

Experiment

As a next step, you might devise an experiment to look more deeply into the problem. A well-designed experiment allows you to isolate the factors you think are important, while controlling or leaving out the rest.

Somehow you have to extract the colored chemicals from a batch of green

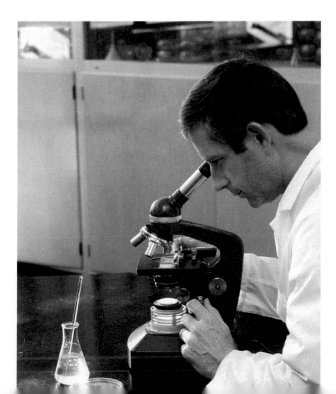

leaves and those from a batch of brown leaves. You might do this, for example, by crushing the leaves and putting a drop of "leaf juice" partway up a narrow strip of blotting paper. Hanging the blotting paper so that it dips in a bowl of water would then cause different colored chemicals from the leaf to be carried to different heights up the paper. By comparing the blotting paper records from the green leaves and the brown leaves, you would be able to tell which chemicals were the same and which were different. Then, depending on the results, you could conclude that your first hypothesis seemed right or that it needed to be replaced by a new one.

Real Science

What we have just described is perhaps the "standard" or "ideal" way to do science. But just as real houses are never spotlessly clean, real science is never quite as neat and tidy as we might wish. Experiments and investigations do not always go the

way scientists expect. Being human, scientists cannot control all the parts of an experiment. Sometimes they are surprised by the results, and often important discoveries are made completely by chance.

Breakthroughs in science do not even have to begin with an observation of the outside world. Albert Einstein, for instance, used "thought experiments" as the starting point for his greatest pieces of work—the special and general theories of relativity. One of his earliest thought experiments was to imagine what it would be like to ride on a light beam. The fact is, scientists use all sorts of different approaches, depending on the problem and the circumstances.

Some important things, however, are common to all science. First, scientists must always be ready to admit mistakes or that their knowledge is incomplete. Scientific ideas are thrown out and replaced if they no longer agree with what is observed. There is no final "truth" in science—only an ongoing quest for better and better explanations of the real world.

Second, all good experiments must be able to be repeated so that other scientists can check the results. It is always possible to make an error, especially in a complicated experiment. So, it is essential that other people, in other places, can perform the same experiment to see if they agree with the findings.

Third, to be effective, science must be shared. In other words, scientists from all over the world must exchange their ideas and results freely through journals and meetings. Not only that, but the general public must be kept informed of what scientists are doing so that they, too, can help to shape the future of scientific research.

To become a better scientist yourself is quite simple. Keep an open mind, ask lots of questions, and most important of all—experiment!

▲ *A Boeing 747-400 jet taking off from a desert runway.*

CHAPTER 1

Amazing Air

A Boeing 747 "jumbo" jet taxis onto the runway, carrying over 350 passengers and crew. Its main deck, 180 feet in length, is longer than the first flight of the Wright Brothers in 1908. Its weight is about 400 tons, including enough fuel to drive a car nonstop for about three years. Yet, within seconds, this monster of metal, fuel, and cargo is in the air. Soon it is flying higher than Mount Everest at a speed of almost 600 miles per hour. How is this possible? How could something so big and heavy fly so well?

An albatross wheels lazily over the ocean, its five-foot-long wings hardly ever beating. Forty thousand feet above it, a Concorde airliner tears through the sky at twice the speed of sound. In just two and a half hours it whisks its passengers from London to New York. All around the world, there are things flying, hovering, drifting, or floating in the air. Some are living creatures; others are human-made machines. How does each of them manage to stay up? How does flight work?

The answer has to do with air and the way air moves around objects.

Some Pressing News

Air is everywhere around us. It is invisible and, most of the time, unnoticeable. But the power of moving air can make itself frighteningly clear. During a tornado or hurricane, trees are ripped up, houses are wrecked, and cars are tossed around as if they were toys.

Air seems weightless. But the air filling your bedroom weighs roughly the same as you do. In fact, all the air on earth weighs about 11 quintillion pounds!

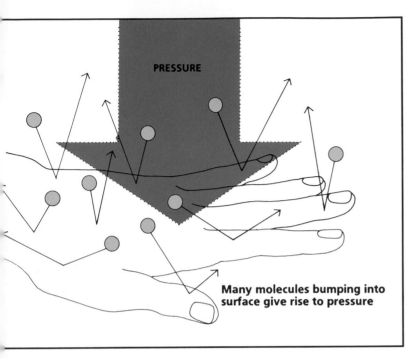

PRESSURE

Many molecules bumping into surface give rise to pressure

▲ *Many molecules bumping into a surface, such as a person's hand, create pressure.*

Like most matter, air is made up of tiny particles called molecules. In solids or liquids, the molecules are packed tightly together. But in gases such as air the molecules are far apart and move very rapidly. The average speed of air molecules in a warm room is about 1,130 miles per second.

When an air molecule crashes into something, such as your hand, it gives it a tiny push before bouncing off again. The

Air on the Move

You Will Need:

- **Two sheets of paper**
- **Two thick books**

What to Do:
Hold one of the sheets of paper close to your bottom lip and blow hard across the upper surface. What happens?

Place the two books about 4" apart on a table. Lay a sheet of paper over the books. Blow hard through the gap between the books. Notice how the paper moves.

Hold the two sheets of paper upright, a few inches apart in front of your face. Again, blow hard and watch what happens.

Try to explain your observations by thinking about the air pressure on either side of the paper in each of the experiments. What did you do to the air on one side when you blew it? What effect do you think this had on the pressure on that side?

effect of just one molecule is far too small to notice. But billions and billions of air molecules bump into your hand every second. That gives rise to quite a strong pressing force, or pressure. Why, then, do you not feel it? The answer is that more or less the same number of molecules are colliding with the other side of your hand. So, the pressure on either side is balanced out.

More Speed, Less Pressure

In 1738, the Swiss mathematician Daniel Bernoulli made a surprising discovery. It has become known as Bernoulli's principle.

Bernoulli found that as the speed of a gas or a liquid increases, its pressure drops. This means that air rushing over a surface, for example, pushes against the surface less than if the air were still.

If air moves everywhere around an object at the same speed, then the pressure on all sides will drop by the same

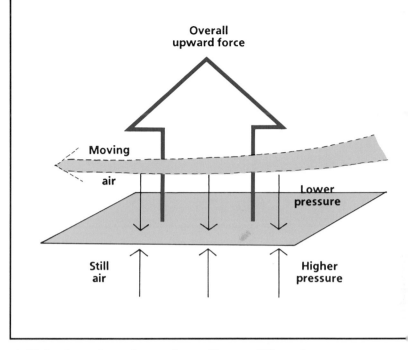

▲ *This drawing shows how Bernoulli's principle results in an upward-pressing force.*

amount. In this case, the pushing force from every direction remains balanced. But what happens if the air only moves over the top of an object and is still underneath? From Bernoulli's principle, it follows that the pressure on top will be less than that underneath. Because of this, there will be an upward-pressing force.

If you have done the experiment on page 10, use these ideas in looking again at your results.

Mapping Air Flows

You Will Need:

- A glass jar
- 20 or 30 pins
- Paper, scissors, and glue
- A large wood or cork board
- A large sheet of paper
- A pencil
- A blow dryer

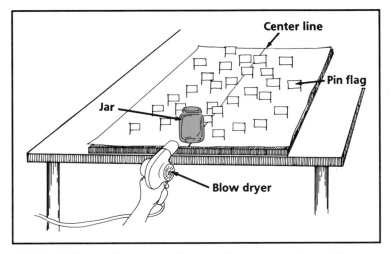

▲ What does this experiment show you about the way air flows around objects?

What to Do:

Cover the board with the sheet of paper. Draw a line down the middle of the paper at right angles to the edge nearest you.

Cut a 1/2" wide, 2" long strip of paper and fold it around one of the pins. Glue the ends of the paper together so that the result is a small flag, with the pin as the flagpole. The paper should be able to spin easily around the pin when you blow on it. Make similar flags using the other pins.

Place the glass jar at the near edge of the board on the middle of the line. Stick the pins in at various points behind and to the side of the jar. Some should be close behind the jar, others farther away. Turn all the flags so that they are pointing inward at right angles to the center line.

Point the blow dryer at the near side of the jar, about 6" away, and directly along the center line. Switch it on to the lowest setting for several seconds. Then turn it off. Look at the new position of the flags.

Under each flag draw a short line to show the direction in which it now points. Then remove the flag. Observe the pattern of lines. What does this tell you about the way the air flowed around the jar?

Taking It Further:
Repeat the experiment with the pins in new positions. For example, you could stick the pins at the ends (or beginnings) of the short lines. By doing this a number of times, you could map out complete lines of flow. Make sure that you hold the blow dryer in exactly the same place each time.

Do the whole experiment again with different shaped obstacles—some with straight sides, others with smoothly curved sides. What happens if you make the surface of the jar less smooth by wrapping it with cloth? What happens if you increase the speed of the air flow?

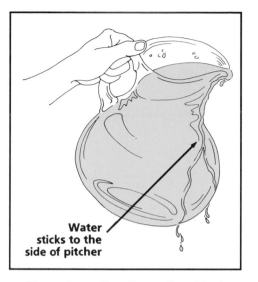

Water sticks to the side of pitcher

▲ *How does the Coanda effect affect the way air flows?*

Sticky Streams

Sometimes when you try to pour water from a jug the water runs down the side of the jug. In fact, all liquids and gases behave this way. That is, when flowing past a smooth surface, they tend to stay close to the surface. The effect was first described by a Romanian engineer, Henri Coanda, in 1926, and is named after him.

Because of the Coanda effect, moving air will try to follow the lines of an object, even if it has to change direction to do so. Now that you know this, look again at any results you have obtained for the experiment on page 53, section 1.

CHAPTER 2

Wings and Lifting Things

Birds and airplanes have one very important thing in common: They both make use of wings to fly.

An eagle and an airliner may not look alike, but their wings are shaped in a similar way. The upper surface of the wing is curved. It rises steeply and smoothly from the front, or leading edge, and then drops away gently to the rear, or trailing edge. The lower surface of the wing, by comparison, is much flatter. Why should this particular shape be so important for flight?

A bird and an airplane in flight both depend on their wings.

A Wind Tunnel

You Will Need:

- **16 large milk cartons**
- **A powerful fan, preferably with several speed settings**
- **A large wooden board**
- **Glue or tape**
- **A sheet of paper (about 8-1/2" x 11")**
- **A knitting needle**
- **Cotton thread***
  Note: Items marked "*" are used only in the "Taking It Further" part of an experiment.

What to Do:

Cut out the front and back of the milk cartons. Glue or tape the cartons together to make a 4-by-4 square, as shown. Fix this arrangement to the wooden board. Place the fan behind the cartons so that it is exactly in line with them. Position the center of the fan opposite the center of the square. The basic wind tunnel is now complete.

Fold the sheet of paper in half. Tape the top half to the bottom half about 1" from the edge. The paper now looks like a stubby wing. Slide the knitting needle into the fold.

Turn the fan on to its lowest speed. Hold the knitting needle level in the center of the air stream with the curved side of the wing uppermost. What hap-pens? Turn the wing upside down and try again. What effect does this have?

Taking It Further:

Tape several pieces of thread along the front edge of the wing so that they trail back over the upper wing surface. Replace the wing in the wind tunnel. What happens to the thread when the air stream is turned back on? What happens if you switch the fan to a higher speed?

Make wings of various different shapes and test them. Record your results and try to explain them.

For suggestions on how to improve the wind tunnel, see "Experiment in Depth," page 53, section 1.

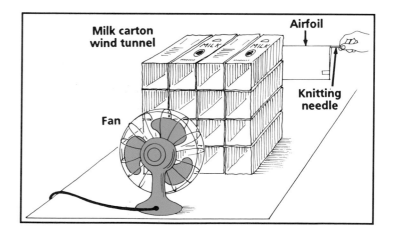

Milk carton wind tunnel

Airfoil

Fan

Knitting needle

Note: The wind tunnel will be required for several other experiments in this book.

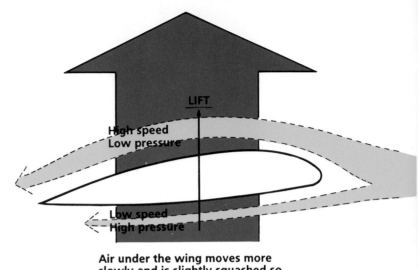

Air under the wing moves more slowly and is slightly squashed so it is at a higher pressure than the air above the wing.

▲ *This drawing shows how the shape of a wing, or airfoil, creates lift.*

Wings and Lift

Think what happens as a wing passes through air. At the leading edge of the wing, the airflow divides. Some air goes over the top of the wing; the rest goes underneath. Because of the Coanda effect, the airflow tends to "hug" the outline of the surface over which it is moving.

The air passing under the wing continues in more or less a straight line. This is because the lower surface of the wing is almost flat. However, the air flowing over the wing has farther to go, because the upper surface is curved. To keep up with the air underneath, the air on top has to move faster. But by Bernoulli's principle, higher speed means lower pressure. As a result, the air on top of the wing must press less strongly against the wing than does the air underneath.

Since the downward pressure on the top of the moving wing is less than the upward pressure on the bottom of the wing, there is an overall upward force. This upward force is called lift.

A wing shape, or airfoil, happens to be the best shape for producing lift. That is why nature uses airfoils in birds, flying insects, and bats, and why human engineers use them in various types of aircraft.

EXPERIMENT!

Losing Lift

You Will Need:

- The wind tunnel
- A paper wing
- A knitting needle
- A stiff piece of cardboard

What to Do:

Set up the wing in the wind tunnel as before. Observe its position in the moving air stream. Now block off the air from the top of the wing with the piece of cardboard. To do this place the edge of the cardboard along the center of the leading edge of the wing so that the cardboard shields the upper surface of the wing. What happens?

Repeat the test with the cardboard blocking off the wind from the lower surface of the wing. What do you observe?

Try to explain your results in terms of what you have already learned about lift.

The Flight of the Frisbee

Scientific discoveries and inventions are often made completely by accident. Take Frisbees, for instance. In 1871, William Russell Frisbie opened a pie factory close to the college that, sixteen years later, became Yale University. Hungry students of the college, who were regular customers, soon found that the empty pie tins flew extremely well when thrown upside down! It was not until the 1940s, however, that someone took full advantage of the idea. Then Frederick Morrison, a keen pie-tin thrower, made a similar disk out of a new type of plastic. Later, he sold his invention to the Wham-O Corporation of California, which coined the name "Frisbee" for the toy.

A Frisbee produces lift in the same way as a wing. That is, the top of the disk is curved while the bottom is flat. During flight, this results in a lower air pressure on

Looking at Feathers

You Will Need:

- A feather (Find one of the long narrow feathers lost from the end of a bird's wing.)
- A magnifying glass or low-power microscope

What to Do:
Look at the feather from the side. What shape does it have? Examine the feather under the magnifying glass or microscope. What do you see? Identify the central shaft and the barbs projecting from each side. Focus on one of the barbs. Attached to each barb are tiny branches called barbules. These lock together—but how? Examine them carefully to find out.

Hold the feather straight out by the end of its shaft. Tilt it so that the front edge is slightly higher than the back. Now move it quickly through the air. What do you notice?

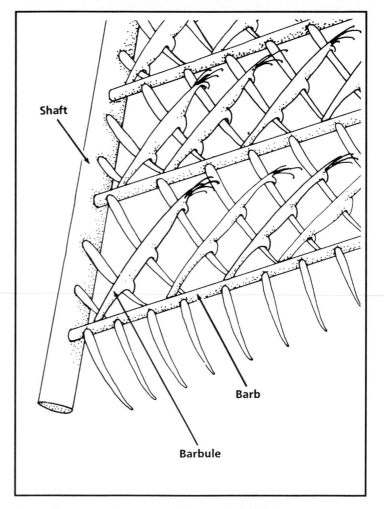

Shaft

Barb

Barbule

▲ *A close-up diagram of a bird's feather.*

top than on the bottom. But the similarity between the Frisbee and a wing ends there. Because of its spin, the Frisbee behaves in a much more complicated way.

Feather Power

A bird's wings, and each of its feathers, are shaped much like an aircraft's wing–curved on top and flatter underneath. This allows them to generate lift in the same way.

The main problem facing a bird—especially a heavy bird—is taking off. To do this, the bird has to beat its wings very hard to force air quickly over the wings' upper surfaces and so produce a lot of lift. Once it has climbed high enough, the rate of beating can be reduced to that needed for level flight.

Several factors help to give birds mastery of the air. They have bones that contain many hollow spaces, making them lightweight yet strong. A bird's chest muscles, which operate the wings, are extremely large and powerful. And, finally, the wings themselves are covered in tightly fitting feathers that trap the air.

Believe It or Not!

ONE BIRD, THE SOOTY TERN, CAN FLY FOR UP TO FOUR YEARS WITHOUT LANDING. IT FEEDS AND EVEN SLEEPS ON THE WING!

CHAPTER 3

Plane Easy!

There is much more to an airplane than just a wing. By some means, the plane has to be able to control its flight. It has to be able to go up and down, and turn to the right and to the left.

A plane must also have some means by which to go fast enough. Only if the air flows over the wings above a certain speed will the lift be sufficient for the craft to leave the ground or stay in the air. In order for a jumbo jet to take off, for example, it must normally be traveling between about 165 and 182 miles per hour. As it climbs, it goes faster and faster, until it levels out at a height of about 32,000 feet and a cruising speed of around 570 miles per hour.

A passenger jet in flight. ▶

Test Flights

You Will Need:

- A piece of stiff paper, 9-1/2" x 5"
- A piece of stiff paper, 8" x 1"
- A drinking straw, 7" long
- Glue and tape
- A pencil and a ruler
- The wind tunnel
- Pieces of balsa wood, styrofoam, and other model-making materials*

What to Do:

Take the larger sheet of paper and make a fold 2-1/4" from one end as shown. Place the long side under the ruler and pull upward to give this side a gentle curve. Glue the back edges together to make an airfoil shape. This is your aircraft's main wing. Cut and crease two small flaps at the back edge of the wing as shown.

At this stage, you may choose to test your wing in the wind tunnel. Read the notes in "Experiment in Depth," page 53, section 1, for ideas on how to do this. Test the wing with the flaps level, with both up or down, and with one up and the other down. What do you notice? What does this tell you about how the wing may behave in flight?

Form the tail by folding and gluing as shown. Cut away the back 1/2" of the tail planes so that the upright flap—the rudder—sticks out. Cut and crease the flaps on the tail planes. Fix the wing and tail securely to the straw with tape. Make sure that the main wing and tail planes are lined up and even. The front edge of the wing should be 2" back from the nose. The back of the tail planes should line up with the rear of the straw so that the rudder overhangs. Fix one or two paper clips to the nose to counterbalance the weight of the tail.

Experiment with the whole plane in the wind tunnel if you wish. Then carry out a number of test flights with the flaps and rudder in various different positions. What happens if you alter the number of paper clips on the nose? What happens if you launch the plane at different speeds and at different angles to the ground? Try to explain your findings.

Taking It Further:

Design your own plane with wings of different shapes and sizes. Use other

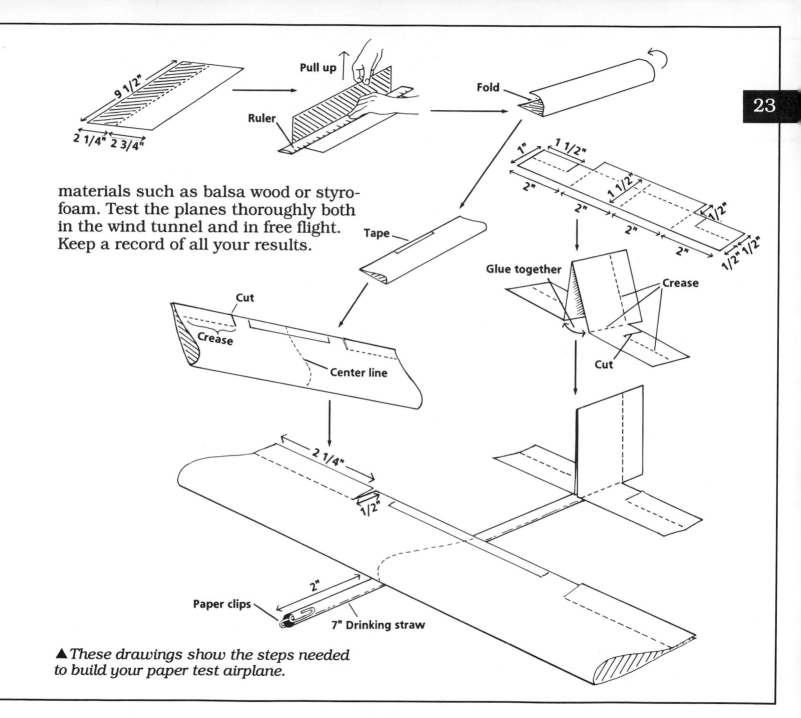

9 1/2"

2 1/4" 2 3/4"

Pull up

Ruler

Fold

1" 1 1/2"

2" 1 1/2"

2" 1/2"

2" 2"

1/2" 1/2"

materials such as balsa wood or styrofoam. Test the planes thoroughly both
in the wind tunnel and in free flight.
Keep a record of all your results.

Tape

Glue together

Crease

Cut

Cut

Crease

Center line

2 1/4"

1/2"

2"

Paper clips

7" Drinking straw

▲ *These drawings show the steps needed
to build your paper test airplane.*

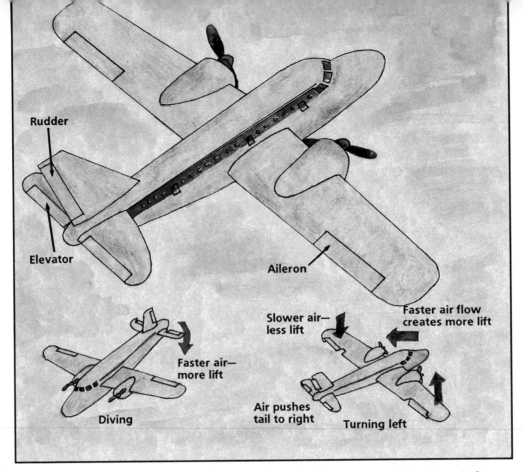

Rudder

Elevator

Aileron

Slower air— less lift

Faster air flow creates more lift

Faster air— more lift

Diving

Air pushes tail to right

Turning left

▲ *Changing the positions of an airplane's flaps cause it to turn left or right and to gain or lose altitude.*

At the Controls

Hinged flaps, called ailerons, on the trailing edge of an aircraft's main wing can be moved up and down by the pilot. If an aileron is raised, this slows the air moving over the upper surface of the wing, thereby increasing its pressure. As a result, the wing has less lift. If the aileron is lowered, the air speed over the upper wing surface is increased, which decreases the pressure. So, in this case, the lift becomes greater.

What happens if the left aileron is raised and the right one is lowered? The answer is that the left wing drops because it loses lift, the right wing rises because it gains lift, and the plane as a whole banks to the left. If the position of the ailerons is reversed, the plane banks to the right. To assist in these movements, a rudder on the tail is tilted to the left for a left turn and to the right for a right turn.

Two smaller flaps on the tail planes at the back of the plane can also be moved up and down. These are known as elevators. With the elevators in the "down" position, the lift on the tail is increased, so that the nose drops and the plane dives. On the other hand, if the pilot puts the elevators up, this causes the tail to drop and the plane to soar.

If you have the chance to visit an airport or to sit near the wing during a flight, watch carefully how a plane's flaps are positioned to control its flight.

▲ *Viewed from above, an airliner's control surfaces on its wings and tail are clearly visible.*

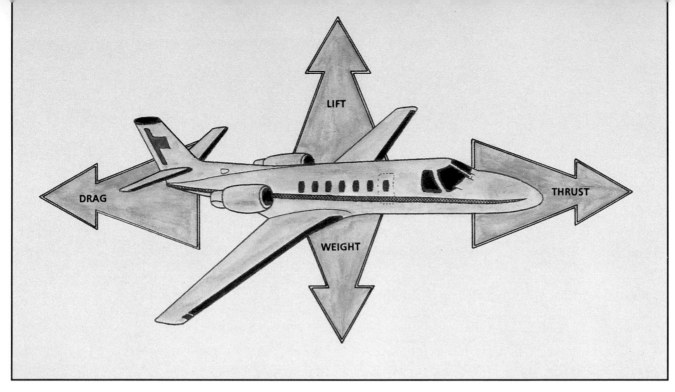

▲ *Four main forces act on an aircraft.*

A Battle of Forces

Four main forces act on an aircraft. There is the lift acting upward and the weight of the plane acting downward. If the lift is greater than the weight, the plane goes up. If the lift is less than the weight, the plane goes down (or stays on the ground). And if the lift and weight are equal, the aircraft continues in level flight.

To move forward the plane must use its engines. These produce a forward force known as thrust. Thrust is needed to make the plane go at a sufficient speed for the air rushing over the wings to produce enough lift. Acting in the opposite direction to thrust is the resistance of the air on the plane's wings and body. This resistance is called drag.

It's a Drag

You Will Need:

- **A tall glass container**
- **Water glass (a clear, syrupy liquid obtainable from drug stores)**
- **Modeling clay**
- **A stopwatch**

What to Do:

Break the clay into pieces exactly the same size. Make various shapes from these pieces. Some will have smoothly curving outlines such as balls, teardrops, or bullet shapes, while others will be more angular or irregular.

Pour water glass into the container until it is about three-quarters full. Drop each of the shapes in turn from the surface of the water glass and use the stopwatch to time how long it takes for each to reach the bottom. Which shapes travel fastest? What does that tell you about the amount of drag acting on them?

Try dropping other objects such as marbles, coins, nails, and so on. Observe carefully how they move.

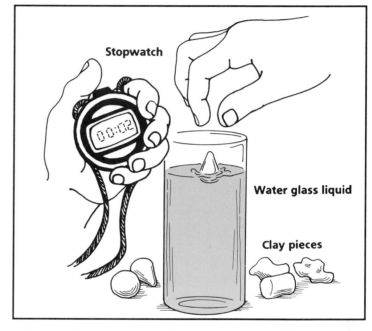

Stopwatch

Water glass liquid

Clay pieces

▲ *What do you learn about shapes and drag from this experiment?*

Warning: Water glass should not be swallowed. Wash your hands and clean up thoroughly after the experiment.

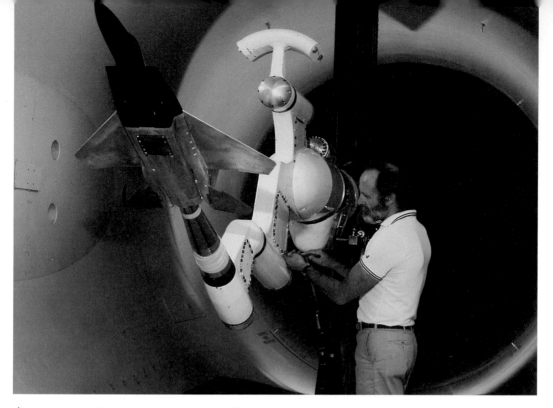

▲ *A researcher tests an aircraft's design in a wind tunnel.*

Streamlining

Engineers have to try to keep both the weight and the drag force as low as possible when they are designing a new aircraft. Using lightweight yet strong metals, such as aluminum, helps to maintain a low weight. But drag is a more complicated problem. Even the slightest unevenness in the surface of a wing or a plane's body can raise the drag force by a large amount.

Using wind tunnels and computer calculations, researchers experiment with different wings, tails, and bodies to find an overall shape that will slip through the air easily, yet still provide the plane with enough lift. A good shape, over which the airflow moves smoothly, is said to be streamlined.

Doing Your Own Wing

You Will Need:

● **Several sheets of 8-1/2" x 11" paper**

What to Do:

Can you make paper planes? If not, have someone show you how. In fact, there are many different ways to build flying models from a sheet of paper. Look for books on the subject or ask your friends if they have any special designs of their own.

Make paper planes with wings of different shapes and sizes—some narrow and sleek, others broad and rectangular. What differences do you observe in their performance? Which planes work best thrown hard and which are better at slow gliding?

A Choice of Wings

Look at the different types of aircraft shown in this book. Look also at the photographs in other books of both military and civilian planes. What do you notice?

Aircraft designed to fly at very high speeds, such as jet fighters, have very thin bodies. Their wings are narrow and swept back. The reason for this is that the drag force acting on an object rises very rapidly as its speed increases. For example, if a plane goes from 500 to 1,000 miles per hour, the amount of drag on it rises by a factor of four. So, it is essential that such a plane offers as little resistance as possible to the air flowing over it.

On the other hand, sleek, sharply angled wings do not give much lift. This is not a problem when moving fast, since the amount of lift increases with increasing speed. But it does mean that high-speed jets need powerful engines to enable them to take off quickly and climb steeply.

▲ The narrow, swept-back wings of these military jets produce less drag at high speed than the thicker, longer wings of a passenger airliner.

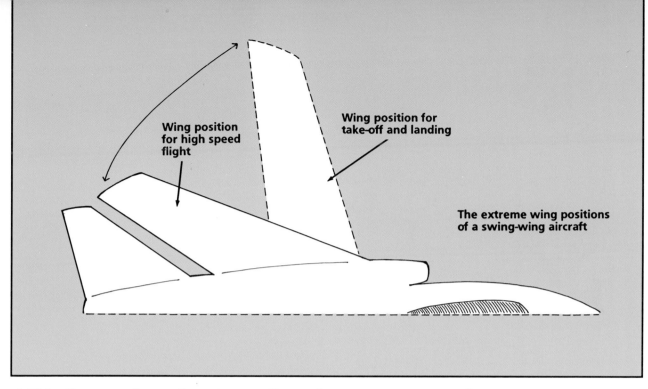

Wing position for
take-off and landing

Wing position
for high speed
flight

The extreme wing positions
of a swing-wing aircraft

▲ *This diagram shows the wing positions of a swing-wing aircraft.*

Planes that are designed to travel more slowly are not so seriously affected by drag. Their wings are wider and stick out more from the sides so that they can obtain plenty of lift even at fairly low speeds.

Swing-Wings

The best of both worlds is a plane that can alter the shape of its wings in flight–a so-

called "swing-wing." One of these is the Panavia Tornado, a multipurpose fighter-bomber capable of bombarding other planes in the air or attacking ground targets. For takeoff and for flying at low speeds, the Tornado's wings are kept straight out from the sides. But as the aircraft gathers speed, its wings are moved into their swept-back position. This greatly reduces the drag on the plane and

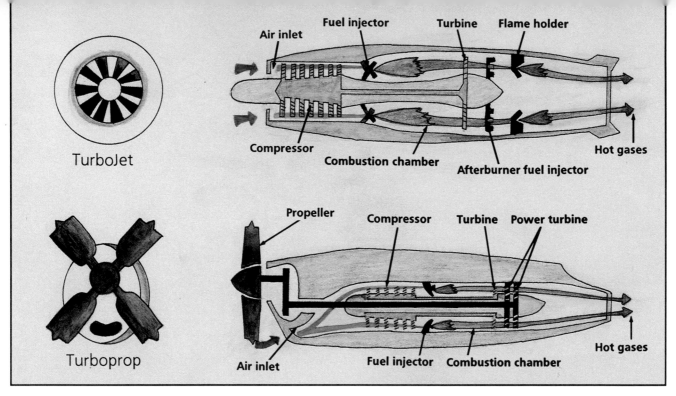

Fuel injector   Turbine   Flame holder

Air inlet

Compressor

Combustion chamber

Afterburner fuel injector

Hot gases

TurboJet

Propeller   Compressor   Turbine   Power turbine

Air inlet   Fuel injector   Combustion chamber   Hot gases

Turboprop

▲ *A turbojet engine* (top) *is much more powerful than a turboprop engine* (bottom).

also allows it to make very sharp turns during aerial combat.

Props and Jets

Until the 1940s all planes were powered by one or more spinning propellers. A propeller is basically just a twisted airfoil. As it spins, it squashes the air that flows over so that there is a higher pressure region behind the propeller than in front of it. Because of this pressure difference the plane is pushed forward.

A jet engine also has a system of revolving blades inside. These make up what is called a compressor. As the blades of the compressor spin around, they suck air in and squeeze it to 10 times its normal pressure. The air then enters a special

chamber where it is mixed with fuel and burned. The hot exhaust gas from this burning mixture shoots out of the back of the jet engine and so provides the plane with a forward thrust. The escaping gas also turns around a big fan known as a turbine, which is connected to the compressor to make it turn.

Being much more powerful than a propeller engine, a jet enables modern planes to fly at very high speeds–in some cases, over 2,000 miles per hour. A jet engine also works more effectively than a propeller at high altitudes where the air is thin.

▲ *A jet engine is tested to see how it performs in an engine test chamber.*

◄ *This new jet engine is a candidate for the U.S. Air Force's Advanced Tactical Fighter (ATF) program.*

CHAPTER 4

Flight with a Twist

One of the problems with most airplanes is that they need a lot of room in which to take off and land. Also, they cannot simply hover in one place. They have to be moving forward all the time so that the air rushing over their wings can provide them with lift.

A helicopter, however, does not suffer from these disadvantages. That is because its "wings" are in the form of a giant horizontal propeller known as a rotor that spins around very quickly. Each of the long, thin blades of the rotor has the shape of an airfoil. As these blades cut through the air at high speed, they provide the helicopter with lift, whether it is going straight up, hovering, flying forward, or flying backward. To move in these different ways, all the pilot has to do is tilt the rotor slightly

Helicopters can move ▶
in ways that a fixed-
wing airplane cannot.

Going for a Spin

You Will Need:

- A square of stiff cardboard about 8" x 8"
- A light plastic thread spool
- Nylon thread or thin string
- A pencil
- A ruler
- Scissors
- Glue

What to Do:

Draw the shape shown here onto the cardboard using the measurements given.

Be sure to mark on the dotted lines as well. Cut out the shape. This will be the rotor of your model helicopter.

Glue the plastic spool to the rotor, being careful to position it exactly in the center. Allow the glue to dry. Bend the rotors down slightly along the lines of the center square. Also, bend the rotors along the diagonal lines as shown. When you look at them from the side, the rotors should have a slight droop and twist that will allow them to slice through the air as they spin.

Wind the thread or string about 15 times around the reel, making sure that the loose end is securely held by the windings. Put the spool onto the pencil, hold it upright, and pull hard on the thread.

What happens if you point the pencil at an angle during the launch? What happens if you alter the amount of droop and twist of the rotor blades?

Taking It Further:

Try making a number of different helicopters, altering the size, number, and folding of the rotors. Which design works best? Can you explain why?

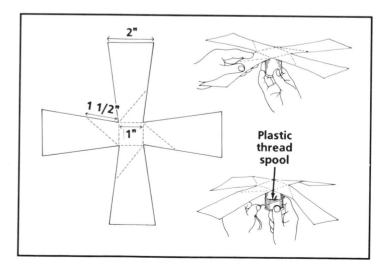

2"

1 1/2"

1"

Plastic
thread
spool

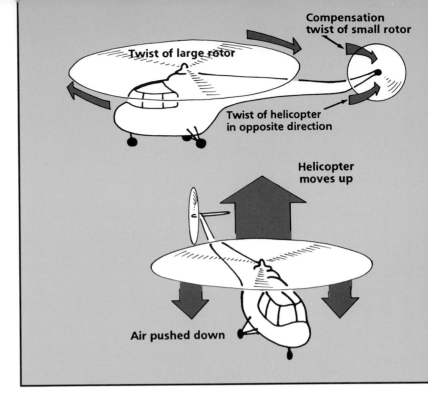

▲ *What are the main forces acting on a helicopter in flight?*

in the direction he or she wants to go.

Helicopters can perform tasks that would be impossible for an ordinary fixed-wing plane. For example, they can hover above a rough sea or the side of a mountain and help to rescue people who are injured or stranded. They can land at special heliports or helipads, even in the middle of busy cities. And they can rush victims of a road accident or other patients who need urgent medical attention to the rooftop landing pad of a major hospital.

An Extra Twist

If a helicopter had just a single rotor, it would be impossible to control. The reason is that as the big rotor spins around in one direction it tends to make the rest of

Believe It or Not!

STUDENTS AT A CALIFORNIA UNIVERSITY BECAME THE FIRST EVER TO FLY A HUMAN-POWERED HELICOPTER. THE WHOLE MACHINE WEIGHS ONLY 97 POUNDS AND HAS TWO PEDAL-DRIVEN ROTORS SPANNING NEARLY 100 FEET. ITS FIRST FLIGHT, IN DECEMBER 1989, LASTED FOR 7 SECONDS AND TOOK IT 8" OFF THE GROUND.

▲ *A new twin-rotor helicopter, the MH-47E, is designed to meet the needs of the U.S. Army's Special Operations Aircraft Regiment.*

the aircraft twist in the opposite direction. One way to cancel out this effect is to mount a smaller rotor facing sideways on the tail. This creates a twisting force that is exactly equal and opposite to that produced by the main rotor.

Another way to keep a helicopter steady is to have two main rotors spinning in opposite directions. This is the method often used on large helicopters that are built to carry heavy loads. A twin rotor helicopter, such as the Boeing Chinook, can generate more lift than an ordinary single rotor craft. It also needs no tail rotor.

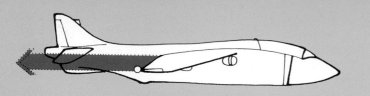

They gradually swivel back until the plane is flying fast enough for its wings to keep it in the air. The process is reversed for landing.

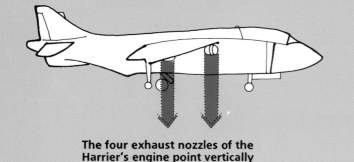

The four exhaust nozzles of the Harrier's engine point vertically down for take-off.

Vertical Takeoff

Not all airplanes need runways. The British Aerospace Harrier, for example, can rise straight up off the ground, hover, and even fly backward! Air, taken in by the Harrier's single jet engine, is compressed and then blasted out of four nozzles, two on each side of the aircraft. For takeoff and landing, these nozzles are angled straight down to provide vertical thrust. Smaller air jets called "puffers," at the tips of the wings and at each end of the aircraft's body, allow the pilot to steady the Harrier when it is hovering. Once the plane is off the ground, the nozzles can be gradually swiveled back to push the Harrier forward up to a maximum speed of 720 miles per hour.

▲ *The four exhaust nozzles of the Harrier aircraft are angled down for takeoff and landing, and backward to provide maximum thrust for flight.*

◄ *A Harrier jet in flight.*

CHAPTER 5

Staying Up — without Really Trying

Airplanes, helicopters, birds, and insects all have to generate a force that is greater than their own weight in order to fly. Yet other objects, such as balloons, seem to be able to stay airborne without any effort. How is that possible?

Why do hot-air balloons fly? ▶

A Lot of Hot Air

You Will Need:

- **Several large sheets of tissue paper**
- **Scissors**
- **Glue**
- **A blow dryer**
- **Cotton thread***
- **A small, lightweight container such as a paper carton**
- **A weight such as a small pebble**

What to Do:

Cut out five sheets of tissue paper according to the measurements given in the diagram. Glue them together as shown. Glue together the long sides to make a rectangular balloon with an opening at the base.

While one or two people hold the balloon upright, use the blow dryer to fill the space inside with hot air. Let go of the balloon. What happens? What happens as soon as the balloon tips over? Try to explain what you observe.

Taking It Further:

Make a bigger version of the balloon. Fill it with hot air indoors, then launch it outside. How high does it go? Repeat the experiment on different days. Does it make any difference whether it is a warm day or a cold one? Why?

For more about this, see "Experiment in Depth," pages 53-54, section 2.

Warning: This experiment should not be attempted without adult help. A blow dryer, like any electrical device, can be dangerous. It should not be used outdoors. It should not be held inside the balloon since this will cause it to overheat.

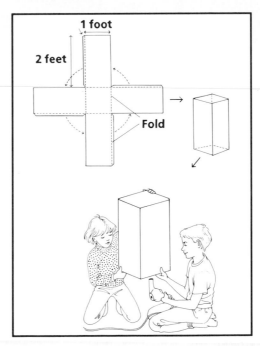

◀ *What can you learn from making your own hot-air balloon?*

▲ *Blimps that fly today use helium to provide lift.*

Lighter than Air

If an object is lighter than air it will rise, just as something that is lighter than water will float. Helium, for instance, is a gas that is lighter than air. So, if a balloon is filled with helium, it will float upward. There has to be enough helium inside so that the combined weight of the trapped gas and the skin of the balloon is less than the weight of an equal volume of surrounding air.

Before World War II, balloons and huge airships known as Zeppelins were often filled with hydrogen, a gas that is even lighter than helium. The problem is that hydrogen burns violently in air. It takes only the slightest spark to cause a hydrogen balloon to erupt in a great fireball.

Apart from helium, the only gas widely used in balloons today is air itself. Hot air weighs less than cool air. Because of this, if the air inside a large balloon is made warm enough, the balloon will rise.

A typical hot-air balloon has a volume of about 75,000 cubic feet, contains about 2 1/2 tons of air, and can lift equipment and passengers weighing over half a ton. The air is heated by special burners to a temperature of about 100° C (212° F). To fly at a level height, the burners are repeatedly turned on for about five seconds and then off for about 20 seconds.

Gliding and Kiting

There is another way an object can remain for long periods off the ground, even if it is heavier than air. This is by using moving currents of air to produce lift.

A glider, for instance, is a plane with very long narrow wings but no engine. It is towed to a height of a few thousand feet by a propeller-driven aircraft (or launched from the ground by catapult). Then it is released. Its wings supply a lot of lift even at low speeds, though not enough lift by themselves to stop the glider from gradually coming down.

To extend the flight, the pilot seeks out "thermals." These are rising currents of warm air that can help carry the glider to a greater height. Many kinds of birds, such as eagles, vultures, and albatrosses, also use thermals to lift them effortlessly high above the land or sea. Notice how the shape of these birds' wings closely resembles those of human-made gliders.

Winds and breezes, too, can enable an unpowered object to fly well. Kites and hang gliders both work by allowing moving air to push against a large piece of stretched material.

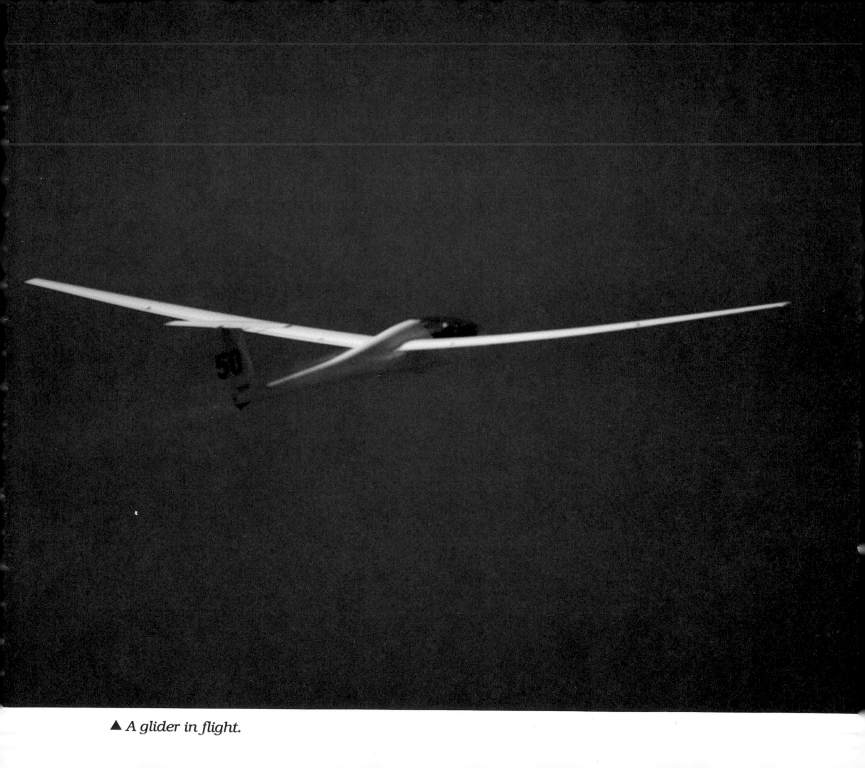

▲ *A glider in flight.*

Windy Travelers

You Will Need:

- A table
- A powerful fan
- A long tape measure
- A stopwatch
- A variety of "airborne" seeds from different plants (for example, dandelion, orchid, clematis, cotton, maple, sycamore, pine, elm, or ash)
- Pieces of various lightweight materials, such as paper and cellophane

What to Do:

Set up the fan on the table at one end of a large room such as a gymnasium. Turn the fan on to its highest setting.

Stand about three feet in front of the fan and drop a seed into the current of air that is blowing out. Follow the seed to find where it lands but make sure that your own movements do not disturb the seed's flight. Make a note of the type of seed, how far it travels from the point of release, and how long it stays in the air.

Repeat this several times for each

A close-up view ▶ of dandelion seeds blown through the air by the wind.

type of seed. Find the average measurements for that type by dividing the total distance covered and the total time in flight by the number of seeds. Continue the experiment with the next variety of seed.

Which kinds of seeds travel the farthest? What do you notice about the way each type of seed moves? Does it spin or tumble in flight? Does it drop all the time or does it sometimes gain height before falling? By looking at the seeds, try to explain the way they move through the air.

Taking It Further:

Try making some "seeds" of your own from various lightweight materials such as tissue paper, cotton thread, cellophane, and so on. Can you improve on nature's designs? Which of your human-made seeds travels the farthest? What happens if you sprinkle a little talcum powder in front of the fan? How far do the particles of powder travel?

For more on this, see "Experiment in Depth," pages 54-55, section 3.

Riding the Breeze

The seeds of some plants are ideally formed for flying through the air. Some, like the seeds of the maple and sycamore trees, are shaped like tiny helicopter rotors. They spin around as they drop from the branches. This allows them to stay airborne longer so that even the slightest breeze may carry them quite far from the parent tree. Why should this be of value to both the tree and the seed?

The seeds of other plants can stay airborne even longer. Dandelion "clocks," for instance, which resemble miniature parachutes, may be carried over a hundred miles in windy conditions.

The greatest distances of all are covered by tiny specks of matter such as pollen grains and smoke particles. These are so light that they can be lifted thousands of feet above the ground by winds or by warm, rising currents of air.

Model Parachutes

You Will Need:

- **Several sheets of lightweight paper**
- **Tape**
- **Cotton thread**
- **Scissors**
- **A ruler**
- **A small object such as a clothespin**
- **A stopwatch**
- **Cellophane***
- **A large cotton handkerchief***

What to Do:

Cut out an 8" square of paper. Tape four pieces of thread to the corners of the paper and tie or tape the other ends to the object below the parachute. Drop the parachute from a high place such as a chair or side of a staircase. Time how long it takes to reach the ground. Take three measurements and work out the average.

Repeat the experiment with 10", 12", and 14" squares of paper. Plot your results (size of paper versus time to fall) as a graph. From your graph estimate how long you think it would take a 16"-square parachute to fall. Test your prediction with an experiment.

Taking It Further:

Repeat the whole experiment using objects of different weight, threads of different length, and parachutes of different shape. Does a circular parachute, for instance, work better than a square one of the same area? What happens if you cut a small hole in the middle of the parachute?

Try using different materials such as cellophane or cotton. Which works best? Try to explain your findings.

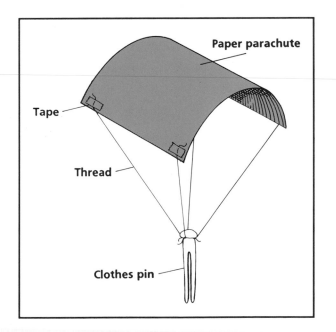

Paper parachute

Tape

Thread

Clothes pin

Dropping from the Sky

The "umbrella" part of a parachute traps air as it opens up. The air is squashed so that it has more pushing power (a higher pressure) than the air around. Since it pushes up, it slows down the parachute and its load to a safe landing speed.

Most parachutes are circular. However, parachutes with special shapes, movable panels, or small openings are often used in displays because they can be steered more accurately.

As well as bringing people gently down to earth, parachutes are also used to break the fall of such things as air-dropped food and medical supplies. Three very large parachutes open up on each of the Solid Rocket Boosters (SRBs) after they separate from the space shuttle at a height of 30 miles. This allows the SRBs to splash down safely in the ocean and be recovered for future use.

▲ *A parachute works by trapping air inside its umbrella-like shape.*

The most faraway parachute will open up in 1996 when the Galileo spacecraft reaches Jupiter. Part of the spacecraft, called a descent probe, will plunge into the clouds of Jupiter at 100,000 miles per hour. A parachute will help to slow the probe's fall so that it has time to send back measurements to earth.

Believe It or Not!

IN 1944, FLIGHT SERGEANT ALKEMADE JUMPED 18,000 FEET FROM HIS BLAZING BOMBER WITHOUT A PARACHUTE. A FIR TREE AND SNOW DRIFT BROKE HIS FALL AND HE SURVIVED.

CHAPTER 6

Faster and Farther

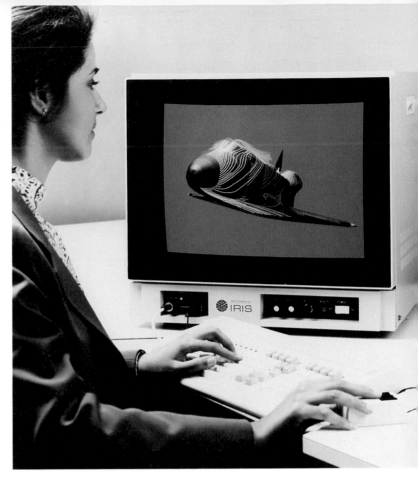

▲ *An aircraft designer uses a computer to test the performance of a design for a new airplane.*

Scientists are always looking for ways to improve aircraft so that, for example, they can fly faster, carry more passengers or cargo, or use less fuel.

Today's fastest passenger plane is the Concorde, which can travel at 1,450 miles per hour or more than twice the speed of sound. Some military planes can fly at over 2,000 miles per hour. In the future, however, there will be aircraft capable of even higher speeds.

Moving very quickly through the air causes a plane's wings, body, and engines to become extremely hot. Because of this, new materials are being developed to replace the metal in certain parts of high-performance jet engines and on the lead-

ing edges of wings. These materials include so-called ceramics, which are as strong as aluminum but weigh only half as much.

Aircraft designers are also making more use of powerful computers to calculate, for instance, the best shape for aircraft wings and bodies. Previously, the only way to test a new design was to build a scale model and try it out in a wind tunnel. This is both time-consuming and expensive. Today, computers allow many more designs to be tested under a much wider variety of conditions. Even so, wind tunnels are always used to check the computer findings.

Space Plane 2000
One of the next great breakthroughs in flight may be an aircraft that can fly into space but take off and land using an ordinary runway.

One idea, being developed by the National Aeronautics and Space Administration (NASA), is for a space plane that would have four different types of engines. The first of these would be ordinary jets that would drive the vehicle up to twice the speed of sound. The air coming into the jets would be burned with hydrogen fuel, carried onboard, to provide the forward push.

▲ *An artist's drawing of the NASA space plane.*

Another type of jet engine, called a ramjet, would power the plane up to 8 times the speed of sound. Then a third kind of jet, known as a scramjet, would operate up to 20 times the speed of sound. By this time, the plane would be at the edge of the earth's atmosphere. The plane would no longer be able to gulp in enough air to burn its fuel. So, the fourth set of engines—rocket engines—would take over. Less than half an hour after takeoff, the space plane would be traveling at 25 times the speed of sound (about 18,000 miles per hour) in an orbit 150 miles high.

Around the World in Nine Days

Americans Dick Rutan and Jeana Yeager became the first people to fly nonstop around the world without refueling in their specially constructed *Voyager* aircraft. They left Edwards Air Force Base in California on December 14, 1986, and returned on December 23. The total length of the flight was 9 days, 3 minutes, and 44 seconds. *Voyager* had flown for 25,017 miles at an average speed of 116 miles per hour.

The pilot flew the plane from a tiny cockpit measuring just 5 1/2 feet by 21

EXPERIMENT!

An Aircraft Competition

You Will Need:

- **Various materials for building flying models. These may include paper, cardboard, balsa, plastic propellers, rubber binders, and so on. The exact materials will depend on the rules of the competition and the design each competitor chooses.**

What to Do:
This is an activity for a large group of people, such as a class or an entire school. It is a competition to see who can design and build an aircraft that can: (1) cover the greatest distance from a fixed starting point, or (2) remain airborne the longest.

The rules of the competition must be decided first, for these set the limits of what entries are and are not allowed. These rules should clearly state if there is any restriction on building materials, method of launch or propulsion, size, and so on. Then the venue and time for the competition must be agreed upon. A gymnasium, for example, would be ideal. Finally, there should be a deadline for competitors to register their entries for the race.

Taking It Further:
For more on this, see "Experiment in Depth," pages 55-56, section 4.

inches while the other crew member rested in a space measuring 7 1/2 feet by 2 feet.

Voyager was designed by Dick Rutan's brother, Burt, who first sketched his ideas on the back of a paper napkin in a restaurant. The aircraft was built using many novel lightweight materials, including graphite (a form of carbon used in pencil leads) and paper. It has a wingspan of 110 feet and can carry 1,550 gallons of fuel that weigh 4 tons.

Believe It or Not!

WHILE FLYING AT TWICE THE SPEED OF SOUND, THE CONCORDE BECOMES SO HOT IT GROWS UP TO 10" LONGER. WHEN A CREW MEMBER SLOTTED A BOOK INTO A GAP IN THE WALL OF THE PLANE DURING ONE FLIGHT HE WAS SURPRISED TO FIND THAT ON LANDING, THE GAP—AND BOOK HAD GONE. THE BOOK REAPPEARED ON THE NEXT FLIGHT WHEN THE GAP OPENED AGAIN.

This section looks at some of the experiments described in this book in more detail.

1. A Wind Tunnel, page 15.

Many improvements to the basic wind tunnel are possible. It would be very useful, for example, to install a fan with a continuously variable speed. This should only be attempted by an adult with a good knowledge of electrical equipment. Similarly a device for measuring wind speed (an anemometer) would be a valuable addition for more advanced experiments. The milk cartons could be replaced by a more permanent array made from thin panels of wood.

Some sort of arrangement will also be needed if model planes are to be tested properly in the wind tunnel. A framework could be built from which the model could be suspended by threads. The threads would need to be slack enough that the plane could rise or fall, or bank to the left or right, but not so loose as to let it go out of control. In practice, this is not easy. An alternative method is to hold the plane steady and tape cotton thread to the areas of interest on the model. The way in which the thread is blown indicates the behavior of the air flow.

2. A Lot of Hot Air, page 40.

Making a successful hot-air balloon takes time and patience. The most important thing is that the skin, or "envelope," of the balloon be very light for its size. Try experimenting with both tissue paper and lightweight cellophane to see which works best.

The ideal shape for a balloon is a sphere, because a sphere has the biggest volume for a given surface area. As a result, a perfectly round balloon can hold more hot air for a given weight of envelope material than any other shape.

The trouble is that a round shape is difficult to make from flat pieces. If you wish to attempt it, you will need to cut out 6 panels shaped as in the diagram. Each of

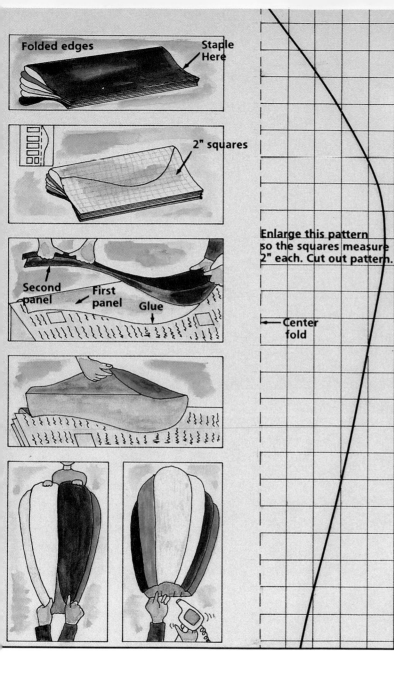

Folded edges

Staple Here

2" squares

Enlarge this pattern so the squares measure 2" each. Cut out pattern.

Second panel

First panel

Glue

Center fold

the panels should be at least 4 feet high. You will also need a circular panel to close off the top.

The larger the balloon, the greater its lifting power will be, but the more heat it will take to sufficiently warm all of the air inside. A blow dryer should not be used outside because of the danger of electrocution.

By means of a small wire basket hung beneath the opening of the balloon by fine thread, the balloon can be made more steady in flight. This helps to prevent the hot air from escaping (though it adds considerably to the total weight). In addition, a small piece of solid fuel may be placed in the basket and lighted to provide a source of heat in flight. Under no circumstances should this be attempted without the help of a parent or teacher.

3. Windy Travelers, pages 44-45.

The type of seeds available to you for this

experiment will depend on where you live. Use nature books or ask someone who is knowledgeable about local plants to obtain more information.

Note that this experiment does not really re-create the conditions of a windy day outside. The fan provides a single, steady stream of air, the strength of which falls off with increasing distance. In the wild, a seed might be blown continuously over a great distance and be subject to wide variations in wind speed and direction. Can you think of ways to make the experiment closer to "real life"?

One possibility might be to actually do the experiment outside on a breezy day. A large open playing field or park would be ideal. While one person releases the seeds from a central point, others might time each seed's flight and measure the distance from the "launch site." Small flags could be pushed into the ground at each landing point, with a different color flag

for each type of seed. This would give a very clear picture of the way in which the various seed types were dispersed.

4. An Aircraft Competition, page 51. This is an activity that might take several hours or several weeks to prepare, depending upon how much effort you wish to put into it. It could be the climax, for example, of a class project on flight. It could involve reading books on model aircraft construction, testing various designs in the wind tunnel, and trying out "prototype" models in free flight.

The most important point is to decide what type of models are eligible for the competition. Are these to be restricted to just paper gliders or unpowered models of any type, or may they include aircraft driven, for instance, by plastic propellers and rubberbands?

The requirements of the models will be very different depending on whether the competition is judged by the distance flown or the duration of the flight. Perhaps a two-part competition could be organized to allow entries in both categories.

A large indoor site for the competition, such as a sports arena, or gymnasium would be better than one outdoors, since even the slightest breeze could have a big effect on the performance of the models.

To enable a fair assessment, each competitor should be allowed three attempts per model with the best measurement being noted down. A prize for the winner, for example, of an aircraft construction kit might encourage extra effort!

GLOSSARY

aileron—a panel on the main wing of an aircraft that can be raised or lowered to help change the plane's direction

airfoil—a shape designed to provide lift when air moves around it

Bernoulli's principle—the principle that when the speed of a gas or a liquid increases the pressure it exerts sideways drops

ceramic—a nonmetallic substance that is light and can withstand high temperatures. New ceramics are being developed for use in aircraft that travel at very high speeds.

Coanda effect—the effect by which gases and liquids tend to follow the outlines of curved objects they flow around

compressor—the part of a jet engine in which the incoming air is squeezed to a high pressure

drag—the force that acts to slow down an object as it moves through a gas or a liquid

elevators—used here to mean panels on the tail plane of an aircraft that can be moved up or down to make the nose of the plane fall or rise

glider—an aircraft that flies without an engine. Its pilot tries to find updrafts of air to gain height and extend the flight.

helium—the second lightest gas. It is safe to use in balloons since it will not catch fire

hydrogen—the lightest gas of all but dangerous to use since even a small spark can cause it to burn fiercely in air

jet engine—an engine in which air is sucked in, compressed, and then used to burn a fuel. The hot exhaust gases rushing out of the back of the engine propel a jet aircraft forward.

lift—the upward force produced when air rushes over and around an airfoil

molecule—the smallest part of a substance that can exist and still have the properties of that substance

pressure—the force acting on a unit of a surface

propeller—a curved blade that, when spun around quickly, forces an aircraft forward. A propeller is a twisted airfoil.

ramjet—a type of jet engine designed to work at high speeds. It does not need a compressor since the very fast-moving air compresses itself as it enters the engine.

rotor—a set of large twisted blades that provides both the lift and the thrust in a helicopter. The main rotor is attached horizontally and the tail rotor vertically.

rudder—the upright panel on a plane's tail that is moved to the right or left to help the plane turn

scramjet—a special type of ramjet designed to work over 8 times the speed of sound and at very high altitudes

streamlining—the shaping of an object so that a gas or liquid will move easily around it

swing-wing—a wing that can be swept back as a plane gathers speed to reduce drag

thermal—an updraft of warm air found over a hot patch of land

thrust—the forward-acting force, supplied by an engine, that allows a plane to take off and remain airborne

turbine—a series of blades that are turned around by the hot gases rushing out of a jet engine. As the turbine spins around, so does the compressor to which it is linked.

wind tunnel—a device used to test the performance of models of aircraft and their parts in air moving at various speeds

INDEX

ailerons, 24-25
airfoil, 16
balloons, 39, 41-42
Bernoulli's principle, 11, 16
Boeing 747 jumbo jet, 9, 20
Coanda effect, 13, 16
compressor, 32
Concorde airliner, 9, 49
drag, 26, 28, 29, 31
Einstein, Albert, 6-7
elevators, 25
Frisbees, 17-19
glider, 42
Harrier jet, 38
helicopters, 34-37
helium, 41, 42

hydrogen, 41-42
Jupiter, 48
lift, 16, 26
parachutes, 47-48
propellers, 32, 33
science: experiments in, 5-6, 7; hypotheses in, 5;
    observations in, 4-5; truth in, 7
seeds, 45
space plane, 50-51
thermals, 42
thrust, 26
turbine, 33
Voyager, 51-52
wind tunnel, 50
wings, 14, 16, 19, 29, 31

About the Author

Dr. David Darling is the author of many science books for young readers, including the Dillon Press Discovering Our Universe, World of Computers, and Could You Ever? series. Dr. Darling, who holds degrees in physics and astronomy, has also written many articles for *Astronomy* and *Odyssey* magazines. His first science book for adult readers, *Deep Time* (1989), has been described by Arthur C. Clarke as "brilliant." He currently lives with his family in England, where he writes and lectures to students in schools.